Harry Eagleson

Pasadena, 1931

Matthias at the Door

BY EDWIN ARLINGTON ROBINSON

COLLECTED POEMS

Avon's Harvest

Captain Craig

The Children of the Night

Dionysus in Doubt

Lancelot

Merlin

The Man Against the Sky

The Man Who Died Twice

The Three Taverns

The Town Down the River

Cavender's House

Roman Bartholow

Sonnets [1889—1927]

The Glory of the Nightingales

The Three Taverns

Tristram

MATTHIAS AT THE DOOR

By

Edwin Arlington Robinson

NEW YORK

The Macmillan Company

1931

TO
RIDGELY TORRENCE

CONTENTS

Matthias at the Door

MATTHIAS AT THE DOOR

I

IF years had been the children of his wishes,
Matthias would have wished and been immortal,
For so he felt; and he was only as old
As half a century of serenity
Had made him. As a man deserving them,
He glowed with honors earned. He was apart,
Because, being who he was, and as he was,
His natural station would inevitably
Be somewhat on an eminence, like his house.
Approachable, yet clearly at a distance,
Matthias was in harmony with his house,
And with all else that interested him.
He was in harmony this afternoon
Even with chaos; and from where he sat,
All he could see was his. There was no sky
In the wood-shadowed and forsaken gorge
Where he was now, but there would be a sky
When he came out. Matthias loved the sun
Better than shadows, and the more for them
When he came out. Down there it was impressive,
If not for long alluring. Mighty rocks,
Like a mis-shapen city that was dead,
Were monstrous and unreal. Trees were afraid
Of them, and to a straightness and a height
That would not elsewhere have been theirs thrust up
Their tops to find the sun. Somewhere above him,

Matthias at the Door

There was his house; and somewhere in his house
Was Natalie. So Matthias had no fear
To contemplate a friendly retrospect
Of a good life with no disasters in it,
And no infirm mistakes. He had done well,
Wherefore he was a good and faithful servant.
God asked of him no more; and he would ask
No more of God than was already given.
He smiled with gratitude, not vanity,
To think of that. A brook somewhere unseen
Made a cold song of an eternity
That would be always cold, and always dark,
And far from his desire. Having a right
To smile at what he would, he smiled at that,
And was content—when he heard, suddenly,
More than a brook. He started and stood up,
Straining his eyes to see what he had heard;
For he had heard the sound of coming feet
That were the uninvited feet of man,
Prowling where none should be. Matthias frowned,
And with an eye not eager met a shape
Approaching him that was at first a stranger,
But soon was one that he might recognize
Without alarm or wrath.

                              "I'm not the devil,
Matthias. I am only a lost dog.
I was too tired to bark. Forgive my trespass.
You are not God, but you are more like God,

Part First

In a few ways, than anyone else I know.
Have you not thought so? All these rocks of yours,
Piled one upon another, if possible,
Would make a mighty monument, Matthias,
Fit for a mighty man. He might be You.
Who knows why not?"

Matthias made a smile
That failed him in the making, and sat down.
"Your compliments are not engaging, Garth,
And you are out of breath. I am not mighty.
It is your discontent that says I am;
Surely not your discretion, or your tact."

"My tact is a lost ornament, Matthias.
Do you see it shining on me anywhere?
I lost it fighting."

"And just when was that?"
Matthias asked. "And for about how long?"
He gave his visitor another smile,
And studied him a little. He was bent,
As only one of those are who have carried
The weight of more than time. He was not old;
He was not older than Matthias was,
Though many would have said another decade
Might have been his to count. He was alive
More with indifference than with life. His eyes
Were all there was of him that was a part

Of the original picture, and they lacked
A lustre that was right. They had seen more,
Perhaps, than eyes of men are meant to see
Of earth and earthy works.

                        "Never mind when,
Matthias. I shall not fight this afternoon.
My presence here today on your possessions
May be explained. There's a place here I like
Better than any other in the world.
I doubt if you have quite entirely seen it,
Though it is yours. Everything here is yours,
Matthias. I admire and envy you,
Some relevant reservations notwithstanding.
Your progress to all this has made a noise
That would resound in a biography.
And have you never thought so? No, Matthias?
I wonder if you always tell the truth.
As near, I venture, as a man may come
To telling it without knowing it—which is harder."

"I cannot understand you, or your mood,"
Matthias answered, looking at the man
As at a gaunt and harmless animal
Performing a new trick. "You have a way
Of holding one to listen, which has been
The worst of your expense. You might have paid
For less, if only you had listened more."

Part First

The trespasser made no reply to that,
Save one of a slow nod and then another,
Till, after gazing at a vast square rock
That filled the distance with a difference,
He leaned and looked Matthias in the eye
With penetrating and obscure affection
That was not love. "Matthias, I believe
That if I were to make a book of you,
I should begin like this. Or, say like this:

"Men would have said Matthias was a man
For men to emulate; and in return,
Matthias would have said as well of them
As evidence and experience, and a tongue
Stiffened with truth, would say of anything
That was not of itself essentially
The living theme. If others were alive,
And had, for reasons hidden in themselves,
An interest and a pride in their endurance
Of an estate precarious and peculiar,
Matthias would not hurt them. He would smile
At them and their mutations and elations,
At their illusions and importances,
And wonder why they were so much in earnest
Over so little. He would not hinder them
In their pursuits or their proclivities,
Or thwart them in their pleasant homely ways.
His landscape would be lonelier without them,
And they did him no harm—knowing too well

[7]

Ever to try. And why should anyone try?
He had some enemies, and no fear of them;
He had few friends, and had the need of fewer.
There was nowhere a more agreeable bondage
Than his was to himself; and where he was,
He was not anywhere else. He was not one
To move unenvied or to fade unseen,
Or to be elbowed and anonymous
In a known multitude. There was that in him
That was not theirs; and that was all of him
There was for them to know. And had a scroll
Been his that held it all for him to read,
Would he have read it, or would he have burned it?
'A mystery might be worse if it were knowledge,'
Matthias might have said; 'and though unlikely,
There may still be surprise.'"

                          Matthias, troubled,
Looked as a child might who had cracked a nut
And found it empty. On his guard again,
He smiled and answered: "Pleasant, if not profound.
If you go on with it some day or other,
I shall be here to listen. You are welcome,
Always, on my possessions, as you call them.
Whatever you are, or not, you are not common;
And that's itself a gift—or a possession."
He mixed with his indifference an indulgence
That made the other say:

Part First

                    "Thank you, Matthias.
I shall remember that I'm welcome here—
And always. Always is not always long.
And I am not so sure of other days
As I am of today. I like this place,
Because it's like the last of everywhere."

Matthias nodded. "Yes, it is like that.
And I should not be here too frequently,
If I were you. There is not light enough.
It is a place to see, and then to leave."

"It's a place worthy of an observation,
Matthias. Do you see that square black thing,
Down there, that's dark and large and heavy enough
To be the tomb of God? Do you see it there?
Do you see anything Egyptian in it?"

"I can see what you mean," Matthias answered;
And a slow chill that was unusual
Crept over him like a thing not alive.
"If it's a tomb, it's an unholy one,
Where I shall never worship."

                        "And why not,
Matthias? If you would seek a present help
In worshipping the gods that are all gone,
Why not as dark a shrine as possible
For seeing nothing and saying prayers to it?

[9]

Matthias at the Door

Tell me why not. You are as much in the dark,
Matthias, as I am. I know the dark."

"Imagine then the gods—or mine, at least—
Out of your knowledge," said Matthias, drily.
"Would you feed others with a fruit like yours?
You cannot; for dead seeds will never grow."

"I shall not try, Matthias; for you tell me
Only what I said first. I'm not so sure
Your God is not down there, for there's a door
Down there that's like an entrance to the end.
You have not seen it yet. There's a dark place
Down there, Matthias. Do you see from here
Two pillars—one on either side? Two shafts
Carved out of solid night, they are to me,
With darker night between them. That's a door
Worth watching; and I've been watching it, Matthias.
I shall go down to it some day and knock.
Shall we go down together and admire it?
Suppose we do. You should see all that's yours
While you are here."

                    Matthias followed him,
But whether for a whim, or for protection
Of an imperilled soul, he never knew.
"There's a way where we go slowly now, Matthias,
But not a long one. If you follow me,
As once, you say, I should have followed you,

Part First

We shall go on together pleasantly,
And with no casualties. Do you see it now?
Only a little farther, and I'll show you
More than you see."

Following silently,
Matthias felt impatience twitching him
To stop, and with it felt a warning fear
To leave this man alone. Alone too long
In such a waste of evil architecture,
A man too fond of ruins, and of betraying
Himself as one, might see more than was there.

"Here's a dark place, Matthias." He heard Garth
And shivered as one who was prepared to shiver.
"Here is a place I like. I live in the dark,
And for a year have done so. Do you see it?
One of these days I shall go there to knock,
And that will be the last of doors for me.
I have knocked on too many, and for nothing.
Why do you stay so far away from me,
Matthias? I am not going to injure you.
I shall not seize you and assassinate you,
And could not if I would. You are too strong.
You are strong in body and soul, yet I'm not sure
That you are sound in your serenity.
Your God, if you may still believe in him,
Created you so wrapped in rectitude
That even your eyes are filmed a little with it.

Matthias at the Door

Like a benignant sort of cataract,
It spares your vision many distances
That you have not explored. I hope, Matthias,
That you may not pursue them ruinously,
For they may come to this—which you consider
Merely a scenery. You will come down here,
Sometimes, because you do not have to stay—
Much as a child goes into a dark room
Intending to be scared. If I were praying,
I should not pray that you be undeceived,
Or be discredited by revelation,
For that would be a waste of your God's time.
You are among the few that are contented,
Seeing the many scratch—as I have scratched,
Only to find an earth with nothing in it
But fool's gold, which is rather less than iron."

"I cannot say that you are doing more,"
Matthias answered, "than improvisation
That failure loves to sing. It's not good music
For one so far along as you to make—
And last, if anywhere, in a place like this.
Since you are candid, I'll be confidential,
And ask why such funereal interest
In my affairs has overtaken you.
Why should the blight of my discrepancies
Be shared so as to vex and agitate you?
Has envy bitten you, and so late as this?"

"Forgive me—I was looking at my door,
Matthias, or I should have answered you.
It's all a matter of shadows. Do you see it?
From here I see a dark Egyptian door—
Which, if it opened, as it will for me,
Might lead you to another. I don't think so,
And am no longer curious. Do you see it?
It's only a dark hole in a dark rock,
If you see only that. You will see more,
Matthias. You have not yet seen anything."

With what Matthias fancied was no more
Than cold annoyance, he said, rather sadly,
"I'm sorry to have bred in you the venom
That you have spattered so vindictively
Over my reputation—which, if guarded,
Will hardly die of it. I am sorry, Garth,
But I should have to be the God you scorn
Before I made you over, or young again.
When we began together, you had eyes
And ears; and you forgot that you had either.
Am I to blame that you are sorry now,
Or if you talk of—doors? The more you talk,
The more will they be closed. Why are we here?
Why do you bring me here?"

                              "Why does a bat
Fly in the night, Matthias? Why is a fish
Ungrateful if you catch him? Why does a bird

Matthias at the Door

Wear feathers and not fur? Why do you sleep
At night, not sure of waking? Why did you,
When we were young together, walk in your sleep,
And scare me in the moonlight when I met you?
Why do you wear that scar on your right hand,
Where you were burned when you saved Timberlake?
Are you sorry that you saved him?"

                              "Am I sorry?"
Matthias asked. "If words are only trash
For you to throw away, why not be still,
And throw them all away?"

                         "Well, I was asking,
Matthias. If you had left him there to die,
You might have spared a man a deal of living—
Which has not been too easy, I'm assured,
And has not been too fruitful, I am certain.
It's all a matter of our congruities.
They make us as we are."

                         "Have yours made you?"
Matthias asked. "You have made yours, I'd say,
A cushion for your malevolence to lie on.
If you are wise, you will come up with me
And out of this—out of this into daylight,
If any such thing is left."

                         "You followed me,

Part First

Matthias, half afraid there was a door
Down here for you to see, and you have seen it.
My house is built, and so is yours, Matthias.
No, I'll stay here in the dark. I live in the dark.
I have been here so many times before
That once more is no matter. So go along
With God, and leave me here with only a door.
Tomorrow will be Sunday, which is good.
We shall not have to work."

                    "You will not work,
Whatever you call tomorrow," said Matthias,
Not oversure that he had said his best.
Feeling two eyes behind him in the gloom,
He clambered back, as he would from a city
Of tombs and shadows in a nameless land
Where there was left one living. As he moved,
A prickling chill pursued and captured him,
And held him—till he saw through trees again
The sky, and then his house that was alive.
The sight of anything then that was alive
Would have been resurrection; and the sight
Of one that he found living was like heaven.
"Is it you, Natalie? Are you alive?"
He asked; and held her shoulders to be sure.
"Whether it's you or not, don't go away."
He closed his eyes in gratitude for light
And love, and saw confronting him again
The silence of a dark Egyptian door.

He blinked, and brushed his eyes with a cold hand,
So to see real a more agreeable vision
Of a slim woman's easy stateliness,
Which never failed or faltered, or was false
To its design. An edible cleanliness
Of countenance that hungry time forgot,
A straight nose, and large eyes that you called hazel,
And a firm mouth, made a face fair enough
To serve, or to be served. Over it all
Was a close crown of hair—a tawny bronze
Of shades and changes. Natalie called it red.

"Where have you been, Matthias?" Half amused
And half afraid, she waited. "I'd imagine
You have been seeing demons—or been walking
Where there are spirits."

                    He looked away from her,
Over his shoulder, where the shadows were
From which he had escaped, while Natalie stared,
Not knowing whether or not to be alarmed.
"I have," he said. "I have been seeing Garth."

II

A CALM untroubled Sunday afternoon
Was always, for Matthias, a good hour
For thanks, and for acquisitive meditation
On who should feel him next and yield to him.
He was no worse than others not unlike him,
And he was worthier far than many of them
Who pelted him with envy or maligned him
With mirrored attributes of enmity
That was not his, but theirs. He did not hate them;
He measured and reduced them. They annoyed him
So little as only to admonish him
To a more capable humility
In his achievement; and a pleasant Sunday,
With daylight fading, was a time prepared
For peace, and for thanksgiving, and for rest.
But there was less today of any of these
Than he had known since he was born. Today
There were new shadows while it was too early
For shadows, and there was a recurring chill
While it was not yet cool or late enough
For any such thing to be. It was so warm
That Natalie, preoccupied and restive,
Was saying nothing till Matthias told her
Where her thoughts were.

                    "And why are you so still,
Now that he's gone? He was not much to you,
Or me, or anyone; and was least of all

To himself. He was a poor defeated soul,
And one for God to judge. I do not judge him.
I'm sorry for him."

       "Why did you send men
Down to that awful hollow in the night,
As if you knew they were to find him there?"
Natalie asked. "When you came yesterday
Out of that place, you looked as if the dead
Had driven you out."

       "Because I came from there
With two eyes following me, and a man's words
That would not leave my ears. They were not words
That we are here to say. I did not know,
Until too late, that one who was alive
Was dead already—which is not uncommon,
Or not unknown."

       "It does not seem uncommon
To me," she said, and sighed. "There are so many
Who are like that, that I have wondered why.
But to creep into a hole and poison himself
In the dark—it was not nice. Were I to do it,
Should I be weak, or brave—in your opinion?
You have opinions."

       "And I hope, my dear,"
He said, with lips that smiled, "that when time calls

Part Second

On you for bravery, it will be for more
Becoming and heroic proof of it
Than going into a hole in a dark rock
And dying there alone. I may have doubts,
And a few fears, but none of them are drawn
To make a picture of you doing such things
As that. O yes, I'm only a man living—
While God permits; and I must have therefore
My doubts and common fears. I have a fear
Of growing old that is unnatural—
One that I might believe my only fear.
I like to live. I would live on with you,
And always. Which a woman, if driven to it,
Might make herself believe a compliment."

She felt his warm proprietary eyes
Admiring and possessing her, and smiled.
"Or you might, after a few centuries,
   Be tired of her, and have eyes for another,"
She said. "We are not old enough to know
   All things; and I'm as happy that we are not."

"I have seen happier faces, if none fairer,
   Than yours today," he said. "Your thoughts are living
Down there too long—down there in the dark, with him.
But he is not there now, and you had better
Be somewhere else. You had better be here, with me.
I like to see you here. You are so fair
To me, sometimes, that I'm afraid of you—

Matthias at the Door

Or rather of the place my world would be
Without you in it."

          "It would be the same,"
She said; "or it would be so nearly so
That only you would see the difference.
The worlds we live in are not very large,
With room in them for only a few faces.
We meet the others, but we do not see them."

Matthias looked away over the trees
That filled the gorge below. "You will have moods
Until you die," he said, "and I am sorry.
They are like summer clouds that make us ask
If more are coming."

          "No, there are no more coming,"
Said Natalie. "It was only that poor man,
Down there alone, where you were yesterday."
She turned, hearing a sound more felt than heard
Of one behind her, and Matthias rose.

"So long as this poor man is out of it,
And unaccused, he'll have his innocence
To travel on," said a melodious voice.
"God help the homeless. I am glad to see you.
Matthias, you are solemn."

          "It's all Garth,"

Part Second

He said; "and I was saying, Timberlake,
To Natalie that Garth will do no harm
To anyone now—unless she thinks of him
Unwisely."

　　　　　"I should not think of him unwisely;
And I should not forget him; or not wholly—
Or not at once." This man who had arrived
So quietly found a chair, and with the others
Looked off across the trees. He had blue eyes
That held a kindly sparkle, not so bright
As it was once, and a face made of wrinkles.
The story of the world was in his wrinkles,
Natalie said, if one could only read them;
Yet they were not the manuscript of age,
Or of decrepitude. He was built straight
And tight, and with a tree's economy
Of slender strength. His face would have been hard,
But for a gentleness that softened it
Somehow to a thin sort of living leather,
Browner than red—a face for women to see,
While other faces waited. "I came home
And heard of Garth," he said, "and was no more
Surprised than you are. I have outlived surprise—
Which is my symptom of antiquity;
For which I beg your pardon."

　　　　　　　　"You had better,"
Natalie said, and made a face at him:

Matthias at the Door

"If I should find myself without an age,
And crying for one, I could almost wear yours."

"No, I am not surprised. I am only sorry."
Matthias looked at Natalie, whose answer
Was nothing that she said.

                              "And why be sorry?"
Timberlake looked at each of them in turn,
Saying his question over silently.

"I am sorry more for leaving him alone,"
Matthias answered, "than for his leaving life
Behind him. There was no purpose left in it,
For him; and I'll assume it was God's way,
Not his, that he was taking when he left us.
I can afford forgiveness, I dare say,
Of all he said to me."

                         "And what was that?"
Timberlake asked. His blue eyes held a laugh
That all his vigilance would not conceal,
And all his wrinkles listened.

                              "It was more,
If I may say so, than was necessary,
And more than I've a reason to remember.
It was the old confusion failure makes,
And will make always—or as long as men

Prefer to fail. I am not judging him;
I'm only sorry that he should make a show
For me, at last, of an undying envy.
I should have said, indeed, that in his envy
There was, till yesterday, a friendliness
That was almost affection. I was friendly,
But I was not his guardian, or torch-bearer.
My own torch was as many as I could carry,
And trim, and keep alive. Seeing him so bitter
In his contempt of God, and man, and me,
I might have wondered that he was not angry;
But now I see that his intent was only
To put me in my place. Poor soul! Poor soul!
When I see folly that has pawned its wings
Hating itself because it cannot fly,
I'd rather turn my eyes the other way."

"You always do, Matthias," Natalie said,
And smiled with a demure impulsiveness
Of one not meaning to be critical.

Timberlake held his lips together tightly,
So that he might not grin, saying at last,
"That was in ways an able argument,
And in ways mostly music. I'm like you,
Matthias, in my not judging those who leave us,
Or those who are still here. Natalie says
I'd better not. And now that Garth is gone,
I'll say to you it will be safe and friendly

Matthias at the Door

On your part to believe that he was friendly—
As I believe he was. In his last hours
He may have lost himself, and his proportions.
For all I know, a fellow may swerve a little
In his diplomacy before he swallows
At once what's left of life. Having heard Garth,
And seen him, yesterday, you may know more
Of that than I. For me, I'll trust the chances.
I shall not go until my name is called."

Matthias, with a sudden inward flinching,
Saw fronting him again, as in a darkness,
A dark Egpytian door. He sighed, and smoothed
His forehead with his hand. "No, Timberlake,"
He said, "we are not waiting for an end
In any dark hole for you. You are not wise
In all ways, and you are not silly enough
To see yourself dishonored and destroyed
By needless failure and futility."

"My sovereign sometimes has a tendency
To the sententious. And why say 'dishonored,'
Matthias?" Natalie asked.

                    "Matthias means
'Unfortunate,' maybe," said Timberlake.
"Our words have our complexions, like our skins.
Accomplishment and honor are not the same,
Matthias; and one may live without the other."

Part Second

"Yes, Timberlake. A man may throw himself
Utterly to the dogs and say to them
That his accomplishment is less than honor.
The dogs would be impressed." Matthias chuckled.

"Of course," Natalie said. "He should say, 'Dogs,
I am not much, but I am honorable.
So wag your tails at me, and do not bark.'
That would soon quiet them."

                           "Perhaps it would,"
Matthias muttered, after a long breath.
"My God! I'm tired of all this easy greasing
Of rusted wheels with soft apology.
Do you think that will make them go again?
If Garth was honest—and I'll go as far
With you as to say that—am I not honest?
Men who are soft will say that I am hard,
Only because they can't make holes in me.
I can see nothing so miraculous
Or damnable in my not being a fool."

"You are not judging him," said Natalie;
"You are doing with him as he did yesterday
With you. You are just putting him in his place."

He came as near to scowling at his wife
As a man should, and said, respectfully,
"Forgive me if I have a few convictions

[25]

As to what we should make of what we are."

"You have a right to them," said Timberlake;
"Though as an errant brother I'm not feeling
Any too sure today of how my doings
May look to a stern eye. If you, Matthias,
Were not a friend of mine, I might by now
Be cheered with your unprejudiced estimation
Of my deserts. I am as honorable
As possible, but you have not seen my house
Which I shall never build."

                          Matthias gazed
At Timberlake and, smiling, shook his head:
"We can do nothing with a man like you
But leave you as you are—to go your way."

"To the same dogs, you think, that followed Garth.
It may be so. Sometimes I'll hear a barking,
And ask how far away the brutes may be."

"Not the same, Timberlake. You are not Garth.
There are dogs, and dogs. If Garth had kicked the first
Out of his way, he would have scared the others."

"Perhaps the others would have bitten him,
And not been scared at all," said Natalie;
And her words had a sharpness for Matthias
That he had never felt before: "I'm not

Part Second

So sure that you know all there is to know
Of dogs, and dogs. It may be that we'd best
Not know too much of what their teeth may do
Till we are bitten. I can fancy them
Following us without our seeing them
And tearing us to death. It's not their barking,
Matthias, that mangles us; it is their teeth.
Garth could have told you. He had felt their teeth,
And he had bled where they had bitten him.
None of us know for certain when the dogs
Are on the watch, or what they are waiting for.
And as for Garth, I doubt if it's as easy
To write his life in saying he was a fool
As you imagine. I can find other names
For one who did much good, and did no harm.
I find a sort of bravery, if you like,
In his way out. Try it yourself, and tell me."
She laughed at Timberlake, who stared at her,
And at Matthias, and in a wonderment
Of premonition. "Never mind me," she said;
"I'm in a mood. Matthias knows I have them,
Or should know; and he knows how to forget them."

"Twilight will be around us before long,"
Said Timberlake; "and I don't see in the dark.
I've had for some time an uneasiness
Of one who has arrived at a wrong hour.
Garth has upset your hive, and all your bees
Are flying about your heads and about mine,

[27]

As active as they are invisible.
You may not hear them, but they make a noise
Like thunder rumbling in another world—
Which may be one where Garth is. So good night,
And wish me joy, for I am going home.
My home is where I take my collar off,
And presently my shoes."

Natalie flashed
A look at Timberlake that he remembered;
And then, remembering it, she laughed. "Good Lord!
Don't go away," she said, "leaving us here,
Or Garth may come between us, like a sword;
Which would be awful, and unnecessary."

"Some of your language is unnecessary,"
Matthias warned her, gently. "Why is Garth
A burden for you now? He won't come back;
And I can show no better friendliness
To him than in my joy that he may not;
For the same life would be awaiting him,
And one more death. For cause that was apparent,
Dying was his career. When a man says
Unceasingly what things he is to do,
Until he says at last he can do nothing,
He meets a desperation."

"Or a dog,"
Said Natalie, "whose name is Desperation.

Part Second

I shall shriek, certainly, if this goes on.
Women are funny, but there's nothing alive
So funny as men when they are telling others
How to put fate in a cage—as they have done."

"I'll set mine free and follow it, and go home,"
Timberlake said, and rose. "When fates are restive,
They let us know. Natalie, you had best
Believe Matthias, and say no more of Garth.
He has gone forward, and that's well for him."

She seized him with a long inquiring look
That was not happy. "How do you know," she said,
"Where Garth has gone? I'd fly for such a knowledge."

He waited there, with his eyes held by hers,
Till all three in the twilight, though together,
Were like three strangers who were there alone.
"I don't," he said. "Good night." And he was gone.

Natalie turned her face to find Matthias
Observing her with eyes that had a light
As kind as twilight. "He might be as far
Away from us," he said, "for all we see,
As Garth has gone. He leaves a loneliness."

"It might be so," she said, "if it were so.
A lonely chair, a match, and a few ashes,
Are like a death, saying where friends have been—

Matthias at the Door

Friends who may not return. They will be there,
Sometime, for the last time. That's Garth again,
Giving me fancies. I must have liked that man.
I'm sorry if I was too unsociable,
Matthias; and if I was, it was all Garth."
She tapped his cheeks and kissed him on the nose,
Which had for years been her best way of saying
That everything was right.

                              She would have moved
Away then, but she failed. She felt his hands
Like iron that held her without hurting her,
And her arms yielded. She looked up at him
With a serenity that bewildered him,
Smiling with eyes in which he could see twilight,
And waiting for his hands to let her go.
She laughed at him, and then she said, "What is it?"

For a long time she waited for an answer
That would not come. Only his tightening hands
Told her that he had heard, until he said,
"Women like you are not demonstrative,
And men like me may not be always vocal."

"If I were too demonstrative, Matthias,
I might surprise you. Now it is you, instead,
Who are surprising me. I'm rather patient,
And have been cherished for my disposition;
Yet, I suppose, if it should have no end,

I might be weary of this. What have I done?
What is it?"

          With eyes unwilling to leave hers,
He watched her while his hands, reluctantly,
Released her prisoned arms. "Nothing," he said.
"Nothing," he said again. "It was all Garth."

III

NATALIE, playing lightly with an envy
Of almost anything not herself alive,
And everything not alive, saw the years coming,
And having seen more of them than were important,
Smiled at herself and wished herself extinct—
Or said so to the cat, who pondered it,
As if in doubt, and went to sleep again.
She sat where they had spoken yesterday
So carelessly of Garth, who in time gone
Had sat there with them and as carelessly
Promised himself the wealth that was for him
His pillow and his dream—not that he cared
For wealth, but for the quieting of some tongues.
Matthias, long familiar with it all,
Had been for years indulgent and amused,
But now for years had nodded, and sometimes
Had yawned. It was his tongue, more than another,
Garth would have quieted. Now Garth was quiet,
Natalie thought, and missed him. She had liked him—
Partly for his futility, perhaps,
Having one something like it as her own
To nourish and conceal.

From where she was
She looked down on the tops of the same trees
That had been there when she had told Matthias
She loved him—which was temperately true.
She did not hate him, and had married him

Part Third

For reasons old as history, and as good
As reasons mostly are when they are found.
"I might have married Garth and starved to death,
Or Timberlake, if he had seen it so,
And maybe poisoned him," Natalie said,
To herself and to the trees. The trees and rocks
Down there were calling her. There was a place
Below those twinkling peaks of oaks and birches
Where men who had been sent there by Matthias
Had found Garth in a square hole, like a door
In a square monstrous rock that she remembered
As one too large to be. More like a tomb,
Where man's hand for a time had followed nature's,
Than a thing there by chance, it would be there
When Egypt was forgotten, and was calling
Natalie to come down to the dark place
Where they found Garth. She was afraid to go,
Which may have been a reason why she went.
"I wonder why we go to see the places
Where those we liked have died," she thought, "and why
We feel as if there must be something there.
I wonder if I'm different from the others
Who are like me."

              Down where the gorge began,
Leaving the sky behind her, she could feel,
Like an embrace of an unpleasant stranger,
The chilliness of an untimely twilight
Surrounding her, and holding her at first

[33]

With no heart to go on. Yet on she went,
And down; and on again and down again,
Until there was a rock that filled the distance
With a square darkness. On she went, and down,
And down, and down, till she could see a blot
That might have been a door, with two dim pillars,
Carved out of night, on either side of it.
And she saw now, knowing before she saw him,
That she was not the only one alive,
There in that place of death.

      "So it is you,"
She said; "and it was in there they found *him*.
Why don't you say you are surprised to see me?"

"I have outlived surprise. I told you so
Last night," said Timberlake, regarding her
With a sad pleasure that belied laconics
Until her silence warned him, and he smiled:
"A normal morbid mortuary impulse
Brought me to see this place, as it did you.
Why should I be surprised? Are you surprised?"

"Never, by you. If they had found you there
Instead of Garth, I should have shed some tears
Of nature, none of wonder."

      "Am I worth,
To you, the moisture of a natural grief

After these years?" He shrugged, and turned his eyes
To the square darkness in the giant rock
Before him. "If I said it the wrong way,
It was because the past got hold of me—
When you and I and Garth, and good Matthias,
Were young and uninformed. Matthias thinks
That he was informed always, but he was n't,
And is not yet—which is good providence
For him, and a good security for you.
The more I think of it, the less I'm certain
There was not too much joy on Ararat
When they all sat and watched the water falling.
It must have pleased the animals."

                         "If it's Garth
Telling you that," she said, "we'll go away.
I'm not a skylark lately, and that hole
Is too dark for a door; and your bright words
Make it no lighter. I have seen the place,
And seeing it is enough. He was in there.
I wonder where he was and what he suffered
Before he found his way there. We don't know,
And so had best be still. Matthias says
Garth was a fool."

                    "Matthias may be right,"
Said Timberlake. "So many of us are waiting
To wear the mark of some such name as that,
That he may throw it where he will, almost,

Matthias at the Door

Assured that it will stick. He's a good man—
Matthias—and you know what else he is.
I love him none the less; I love him more
Than you do, Natalie. He saved my life,
But that's not why. You see, I'm sorry for him,
Which is one reason. There are other reasons,
And they are things of nature—like those tears
You might have shed for me. Matthias needs
As many friends now as there are commandments,
Or more than any man has. Once he had two,
One of them being Garth—for what he was;
Now he has one—for what he is—in me.
The miracle is, he cares. Why should he care
For what is left of me? . . . What—who is this!"

Natalie, while he asked, was in his arms—
Where she would stay or fall. He felt her there,
Clinging and shaking in a desperation
So long imprisoned that escape at last
Was only to another. Timberlake
Held her and wondered what her life had been
To break like this, while a great helplessness
Humbled and stung him. She was his to take
Or fly with, if he would. He had known that;
And there was more than that. He kissed her mouth,
And face and eyes, and held her closer to him,
Remembering why it was he was alive,
And at whose peril. Then she freed herself,
As if in anger, and stood looking at him,

Part Third

Her mask of resignation all washed off
With tears. " You know," she said, "we are two ghouls,
Coming down here like this to watch a hole
Where a man died. Worse yet, we are two fools.
I hope you are beginning to know that."
She sat down on a rock and laughed at him
Like an unhappy witch, with a warm face
That was itself a witchcraft.

                                    " It's not easy
For me to be a scholar, with you near me,
And never was." He leaned against a boulder,
And for a time saw nothing but a face
Below him, looking up, and seriously
Said nothing, till he found a few poor words
That had a wealth of melancholy truth:
"There was too heavy a credit on his side,
And there was little on mine; we'll say enough,
When added carefully, to make a sum
About as large as ordinary honor—
Which, if it's all we have, is more than . . ."

                                    "Say it,
Say it," she said. "Say it is more than love,
Say it is more than happiness, more than life.
Say it is more than everything else together;
And I'll say, when you're done, we are two fools.
Down in me somewhere I'll agree with you,
And then I'll say again, we are two fools.

Matthias at the Door

It does me good to say it, and I enjoy it.
You should have married me, and tortured me,
And got drunk, and left me for other women,
And then come back when you were tired of them.
I should have been the devil and hated you,
And scratched, and made fur fly all over the house,
And loved you, and one day I might have killed you,
And then myself. That would have been all right.
We should have killed each other, and so known
That we had lived a little before we died.
Can you see there no comfort? What do you see
In this? It looks to me a waste of being,
And a more desolate foolishness for knowing
Just what it is." She looked up at him, smiling,
With tears running unhindered from her eyes
And down her cheeks, like little brooks. "Matthias
Would be surprised at this, if you are not;
And I should tell him. There isn't so much to tell,
More than to say we are three fools together,
Each in a crumbling foolish human house,
With no harm done—save two of them in ruins,
And one of them built happily on a lie.
He thinks I love him, and so throws away
No time or pride in asking why in the name
Of heaven and earth I shouldn't. That's his way.
He married me and put me in a cage
To look at and to play with, and was happy—
Being sure of finding me, when he came home,
With my face washed and purring. Poor Matthias!

Part Third

He says I'm not demonstrative, God bless him,
And he says prayers because I'm not a fright.
He's a good man, and has been good to me—
But what if many a man like him should learn
Some things that many a man must never know?
Now look at me, and say, to comfort me,
That I'm a fool. You know that you are one—
Honor or not." She made a face at him,
And rubbed her eyes with a wet handkerchief
That was by now almost invisible.

He watched her, fancying she was like a child
Who had been crying and was tired of it;
But that was no long fancy. "I'm afraid,"
He said, "that he may soon learn some of them.
Garth, I've a notion, tore a few farewell holes
In the rich web of his complacency,
Letting some truth come in. Whether Matthias
Would see the truth, or would see only holes,
Is a new question. I'm not answering that,
But there's an answer, or say half an answer,
For one of yours—if yours was ever a question.
You know the story in a distant way,
And I would rather never bring it nearer.
I don't mind what you call me, or mind saying
That all your names will be as true as tar;
Yet in my wilderness I'd like to save
One refuge for reflection and escape.
While you were speaking I saw only your face;

For there was nothing else—until it melted
Into time going back, and I was there
Strangling, in that accursed house again,
Roused out of heavy sleep by knocks and yells
To find myself there swimming, it seemed, in smoke
Too thick to breathe. I knew there was a door
Where I should never find it; and I drowned
There in that ocean of death-heavy smoke
While it was battered in. All I could see—
While I could see—was red light and more smoke,
And hardly much of either. Light went out
Entirely then, and all remembrance of it,
Until I was awake in a dark room,
And heard Matthias. He was asking for me,
And there was friendship trembling in his voice,
As memory will in music we have heard
Somewhere before. I forget many voices,
But not that voice of his, or what it said,
There in the dark."

              "No, you must not forget it,"
Natalie said; "and you must not forget,
If ever you learn, to tell me why it is
Our fates and ways are so malignantly
Mixed up that it's a miracle to me
So few of us die crazy. I can see
What's coming for you to say. It's all I've seen,
Or guessed, for twenty years."

Part Third

"I know," he said,
And with unanswered eyes he watched the place
Where Garth had been, as if in envy of him.
"There's a malignance in the distribution
Of our effects and faculties. It is nature,
And our faith makes it more. If it's no more,
Garth waited longer than was logical
For a good atheist who believed himself
And life a riot of cells and chemistry —
If he believed it. You say you believe it,
But in that curious woman's apprehension
Of yours there broods a doubt that frightens you
More than annihilation."

                              "The last thing
To frighten me would be that," said Natalie.
"It's only that I have never been quite ready."

Timberlake only smiled. "Well, to go back,
When I awoke there was night everywhere.
If I had eyes, I knew they were on fire,
And of no use to me. I heard Matthias,
And only wished that he had never found me;
More of me than my eyes had lost all seeing;
And when my eyes returned I saw Matthias,
All scorched and swaddled, and so happy to see
That I could see, that I was sorry and sick
For wishing in the dark. Don't wish in the dark;
Or never until you know there's no more light,

Matthias at the Door

Which is a difficult knowledge. If you tell me
You know what's coming of what I'm trying to say,
I'm willing enough you should. I knew Matthias
Had found that my unworthiness of you
Was like an apparition stalking always
Between him and your love. Yes, you are right:
I made myself more worthless than I was—
For his sake, and, as I saw then, for yours.
I don't know what it is that I see now.
If you were not the world and heaven together
For him and his complacent faith in you,
There might be some escape, or compromise
With fire-born obligation even like mine;
Or a maybe-beneficial cataclysm
Might be the best way out, but I don't know it.
Whether my one way then was folly or fate,
Is more, no doubt, than I deserve to know;
Only, I know that I am glad somewhere
Within me, where so little deserves a wreath,
For one thing right—or not. Fire leaves a mark
On friendship that would be a brand on love,
Always in sight; and even without Matthias,
You might have paused. If you had come to me
For happiness, you might well have murdered me,
As you so playfully have intimated.
I should have tripped and slipped and broken the eggs
Until you might have starved yourself to madness.
There's no slight fire in you, my child; and time,
Developing combustion, might have achieved

Part Third

An earthquake, or a woman-quake, within you
That would have blown our problematic house
To chips and flinders, and ourselves as well;
Which would have been more picturesque than pleasant,
More ruinous than unique. The same has happened;
And I have helped, and burned my fingers helping,
To rescue out of hot and smoking ruins
A few things yet worth saving. It's dark work,
And mostly smoke and ashes. Half the grief
Of living is our not seeing what's not to be
Before we see too well. You have Matthias,
And a safe nest. I'm ready enough to know
How far that is from nothing."

                       Natalie laughed,
And dug holes in the air with nervous fingers.
"When you poor men look in from the outside
With your well-meaning and unmarried eyes,
And see so much, and tell us all about it,
What has a woman left to do but laugh —
Unless she cries? I'm tired of crying now,
And tired of this unearthly place. Come here."

She reached up for his hands and drew him slowly
Down on his knees, and having him there, surprised him,
Who had outlived surprise, by seizing him
And holding his hot lips with hotter lips
That had alive in them the fire of death
To burn him till he knew what he had lost,

[43]

And might have thrown away. Slowly at last
There was an end of that, and she sat gazing
At the black rock that she had come to see,
A rock with a dark entrance like a door.
He lifted her and held her while she pointed,
Like a child frightened, at the place where Garth
Had entered and had stayed. "He was in there,"
She said; and they went silently together
Away from there, together and each alone,
Climbing to find a sky.

                    Another twilight
Found Natalie, still alone, where she had seen
Matthias in his chair, and Timberlake,
Who would not come tonight. Matthias came,
As always, and as never before; for silence
Came with him, and attended him along
The dim veranda, where he passed her twice,
And twice again, before he stopped and said:
"You chose a merry place for love, you two,
Down there this morning. You should have gone in
Where Garth went—where there was more privacy."

Natalie waited, but he said no more
"I see, Matthias." Hesitating only
A moment, she stood up, and without fear
Or care for any danger or disaster,
Said calmly: "You had better know, Matthias.
I'll be direct, and so not like a woman

Part Third

As to astonish you, but you will know me.
It's not so dark here that you cannot see me.
Whether you went before me, or came after,
This morning, is no matter. You were there.
Whether you saw me distantly or clearly,
Whether or not you heard me, is no matter.
So long as you were there, that's everything.
I went without a wish and with no fancy
That I was not alone, and found him there.
He was there to see that place. He was drawn there,
As I was; and what followed was my fault,
If it was anyone's fault. You saw me there;
And if you heard me, you heard all there is.
There is no more; there'll never be anything more.
There was a man I would have married once,
And likely to my sorrow, but you saved him
Out of the fire—and only saved yourself
By mercy of a miracle. You were brave,
Matthias; and because he was your friend,
That man gave me to you, first having given
Himself to folly, and to waste worse than crime.
I don't know yet whether he loves me really,
Or if it's in him to love any woman
Save as a game and an experience.
I know that I'd have given myself to him,
Not caring whether or which. But it was you
Who saved him from the fire, and he remembers,
As he remembered then. He is your friend,
And sometime you may know, wherever he is,

Matthias at the Door

Your need of him. I married you, Matthias,
Because I liked you, and because your love
Was too real to be tortured, and because
There was no better thing for me to do.
Houses are built on more infirm foundations
Than ours, and some of them are standing well.
I would not have you walking in your sleep—
Not after this—as you have said you walked
When you were young. Were we ever young, Matthias?
It must have been a long, long time ago.
You see me as I am, and have been always.
I am not lying to you. Do you believe me?"

Matthias, like an image in the gloom,
Stood silent, looking only at the floor,
While Natalie felt creeping from his eyes
Tears that she could not see. It might have been
For minutes or for hours that he stood there,
And she stood watching him. "Yes, I believe you,"
He said, and stumbled as he walked away.

IV

NATALIE, now alone with hours and days
    And nights, found a soul-wearing company
For loneliness in their continuance
To no end she could see. There was no quiet
In silence that was only a slow dread
Of when it should be broken, and no comfort
In waiting for the coming of a man
Whose joy of long serenity and content
Her words had killed. It might as well be so,
She reasoned; for the best and blindest faith
Is dead when it may be deceived no more.
There was no purpose left in her not saying
She was alone; for when Matthias came,
Sooner or later, she would be as far
From him as she had been from Timberlake,
When they had climbed that morning, and together,
Out of that perilous place to find a sky
Above them and a world that never should be
A world of theirs. Now she had found another,
And one that would be hers, and cruelly hers,
While she was in it. Timberlake had left it;
Matthias would never recognize or find it
When he came back. His was another place,
Not hers to enter—and a lonelier place,
Perhaps, than hers; and she had made it so.
Matthias had been told, and he was gone—
Not saying how far away, or for how long,
And his new world was with him where he was.

Matthias at the Door

Natalie thought of that, and of a love
Too real, she had informed him, to be tortured,
And all for this. He had not soiled his love,
Or made possession cheap, or flaunted rights
Of ownership that would have smeared respect.
He knew his way with her amenities,
As with men's power and worth in his affairs
And traffics. There was much good in Matthias—
If only one could love him. One man did,
In his man's way, and Timberlake was gone.
He was not coming back. The mark of fire
Was on his friendship, and was on his love
For Natalie—if it was love. She doubted
If he knew what it was, and would have given
Herself to doubt—her love being more than doubt,
Or death.

      Matthias, coming silently,
As he had gone, found Natalie as fair
And undisturbed and undemonstrative
As he had left her. The one change he found
Was in his world, which he had taken with him
And brought home with him. It was an incubus—
A thing to be acknowledged and endured,
Like an incurable new malady
Without a name, an ill to be concealed
And never mentioned. Once on a time a world
With one man in it might have been amusing
And harmless in imagining, like a sea

Part Fourth

With one fish in it somewhere; but he found
No peace or privilege now in contemplating
Any such world or sea. He was alone—
Alone as he supposed no other man
Was ever alone before. He had read books
About the foiled and the unsatisfied,
Who should have had more sense, and he had known
Many, like Garth, who had succumbed and fallen
Rather than work and climb. But never before
Had he perceived among the foiled and fallen
An adumbration of one like himself,
And would not yet perceive it. He was apart,
As he had always been; and though alone,
He would be always on an eminence.
Natalie should know that.

                      Like one who knew it
By listening unrevealed and hearing him
Through silence, he could see her coming now,
All as if nothing in the world had happened
That had not always been. "I think, Matthias,"
Natalie ventured, "patches are better than holes.
I'll ask you if my notion is a good one,
Or just a preference—or an intuition.
I feel it as a good one. A ship sinks
If it has holes in it that are not patched—
And even in calm weather, like today.
I should hate shipwreck on a quiet sea,
Matthias; and heaven defend us from a storm.

[49]

Matthias at the Door

If I had wronged you or been false to you
In more than thought, there would be reefs and havoc
All round us, for I know you. But is thought
So fierce and unappeasable a monster—
When it is only thought? How many good men,
Like you, are told of all their wives are thinking?
Most wives are full of thoughts. O yes, they think,
Matthias, and mostly nothing comes of it.
I don't say always. I'm saying that my wishes,
If they are strong enough, will hold our ship
Together for some time yet, with only ourselves
To know that underneath, where none may see them,
There are some patches to keep death away.
Matthias, if only your bewildered pride
Would lend its eyes to your imagination,
You would see ships afloat with patches hidden
That would be worse and larger far than ours
Would have to be. Meanwhile I see dark water
Filling our ship; and it's for you to say
Whether or not we sink. I'd rather we sailed,
With a flag flying."

          Matthias, who had scowled
And looked away while he was listening,
Saw facing him the picture of a woman
No longer his. Her body and her face
Would always be as fair to see as ever,
And only fair to see. The woman herself
Was not for him, and never had been for him;

Part Fourth

And it was to that woman he had said
Garth was a fool. A knife was hurting him,
But he made out to smile: "Yes, I suppose
We'd better sail, with a flag flying—somehow.
To sink would be conspicuous and dramatic;
And drama is a show that's always played
By someone else. Yes, we had better sail."
His face grew hard again, and he was gazing
Over the shining tops of oaks and birches,
Growing out of a gorge that held a darkness
That was like memory.

     "I am glad you say so,"
She said, and with a sigh repeated it,
Wearily to herself. "If I could find
Your God, or what you call it, to believe in,
Matthias, I could praise him for creating
A world no worse than this. He might have done it,
If he had tried, and how much worse a mess
We mortals might be making of ourselves
Is only for him to say." With a faint music,
Like that of a cold shadow-hidden brook
Down there that he remembered, she was laughing.

He turned, and after frowning, smiled at her
With a sad patience. "If my faith went out,"
He said, "my days to be would all be night—
A night without a dawn, and with no lamp.
You should know that. God knows you should know that."

"Praise him for what there is, then, if that's true,"
She said. "We might have lost our arms and legs,
And then our eyes and ears. There's possible fate
Far worse than this, though you believe there is n't,
Or make believe. If I know anything well,
I know you'll praise your God, in retrospect,
That all there was of me surviving truth
And revelation was as clean as ever.
No other man has had it, you will say,
And walk the straighter for it. Is that nothing
To you, and your Olympian pride, Matthias?
Is it not even a patch for our poor ship?"
She said it with a quick commiseration
That was a quick regret. Some other man
Might have said vanity was not compassion,
Envenoming an error with a pity
That might be worse.

                    With nothing else to do,
She gave herself to time, and lived with it
As a child might have lived with a dumb mother,
Present, yet never seen. She went no more
Down there, but she would see from where she was,
Darker for shadows always over it,
A black and giant rock that made her think
Of Egypt, and lost sorrows in the night
Of ages, where defeats were all forgotten,
Dreams all a part of nothing, and words all said.
There was a man she had found watching it

[52]

Part Fourth

That morning, but he was not watching now—
Not there. She would not find him there again;
And Natalie, in a broken way, was glad
For one thing in him that she might admire,
While she could only love the rest of him
More than her life. If there was folly in that,
Greater than love, folly stronger than death,
Her penance was to nourish it alone
With cold estrangement and a patient sort
Of rage. If Garth had been a fool, she thought,
What name would poor Matthias find for her?
Had he known all she knew of her deceits
To please him into loving the defects
Of her necessities, he would have lost his wits
Finding a name for her. If he knew all,
He might know more than was in any name
To tell him, and be sorry for all women
Who lie because they live. No friend of hers,
Or garrulous acquaintance envying her,
Would have said everything was not as always;
And time went by.

          And as it went, Matthias
Upheld a dignity that had a distance
Becoming in his new part, which he was playing
Because there was no other. He sustained
His eminence as he might, and to the town
Presented as untroubled and unaltered
An aspect of achievement and address

Matthias at the Door

As ever, and with only himself to know
The sorry toil it was, and Natalie
Partly to know. He might have played for years
To men's indifference and to Natalie's
Unheard applause, if time had honored him
So long. Time was a traitor to Matthias,
Who had believed in time and trusted it
Without a fear of its betraying him,
As faith will trust a grave without a promise;
And in their way Matthias and his pride
Were traitors—if an insurrection sleeps
While its indignities and inspirations
Are moving and awakening in the dark.
Meanwhile Matthias and his pride progressed
With time through hardness and civility
Into a mellowness that Natalie
Felt was unripe. An early-fallen fruit
With a worm hidden in it might have had it;
Or a determination to be kind,
After long injuries and indecisions,
Might have been like it. Call it this, or that,
Or welcome it, it was not like Matthias.
It was too smooth and soft on the outside
To be Matthias. It was not Matthias,
Natalie said; nor was it, mercifully,
A variation of a mortal silence
Which had so long resisted and ignored her
As to be like death dwelling in the house,
Waiting his hour to be revealed and feared.

Part Fourth

It mattered less to Natalie what it was
Than that it should be visible, and be change.

"If it had looked at me, and said something,
   I would have held my hands out to a ghost,"
She said, with a sharp humor, "and embraced it."

"I say with an experience," he said,
"It might have been a disappointing armful."
He took her in his arms for the first time
Since his awakening; and he found her there
No less responsive than a ghost had been,
Nor more for being real. "You are no ghost;
And that's as far today as I have knowledge.
Will you say what you are?" He would have held her
More closely, but she stood away from him,
While he was holding her.

                              "If you surprise me,
Matthias, I may not like you, or believe you.
Like someone else, we have outlived surprise,
Or surely should have conquered it by now."
She smiled a little sadly at herself,
And looking up, saw passion in his eyes—
Passion and sorrow, and a burning pain
That found her memories.

                              "Nothing in you," he said,
"That was, and is, will be outlived in me.

No, nothing." Breathing hard, he let her go,
Leashing her with his eyes, and holding her
From going far. She was too sorry for him
To leave him there alone, or so she thought.
She fancied, for a moment, she was seeing
Their melancholy drama as he saw it,
And pitied him. Pity is like a knife,
Sometimes, and it may pierce one who employs it
More shrewdly than the victim it would save,
And with a wound unhealing.

                              Natalie,
Weighing herself with justice, found a void
Between her and uncompromising earth,
Whereto she had returned, reluctantly,
With pity, and with renewed acknowledgment
On her side of defection and deceit —
Not of itself so much an injury
As a convenience, and a way prepared
By circumstance to make Matthias happy.
That was at least a way of saying it.
She needed him, and there was nothing new
To an old world in her not loving him;
And all would have gone well if Garth had lived,
Or gone more quietly through another door
Than one down there that she was always seeing —
Before her, in a darkness. Time would have held
Timberlake and Matthias and herself
Always the same as they had been before,

Part Fourth

And they would never have been down there together,
Down there among the shadows, where disaster
Was hiding to destroy them.

                              Natalie cried
One day, as never before since Timberlake
Had vanished; and her misery, she discovered,
Had in it more of rage and self-contempt
Than sorrow. She had seen more with her eyes
Of late than with her pity or resignation;
And after two years with another man
Than one that she had married as Matthias,
She had come surely and unwillingly
To see how much of her was left for him
To cherish or believe since he had learned
How little there was before. She could see change
Writing a sordid story on his face,
And she was hearing now another language
That he was learning. An intangible,
Untarnishable seal of something fine
Was wearing off; and in his looks and words
A primitive pagan rawness of possession
Soiled her and made her soul and body sick.

After another year, she felt impending
More than was hers to bear. All she had left
Was a long-vanished presence of a man
Far off, if anywhere, who remembered her,
If he remembered, only as one forsworn

And far behind him. He was not coming back.
There was inviolate fire between his life
And hers; and she was never designed for flight,
Alone, to a new loneliness.

                              Matthias,
With a full, flushed, deteriorated face
That made her shrink, invaded moodily
Her thoughts and fears, and her uncertainties
Darker than any fear. "What's it about?"
He asked; and smiling like a sultan, watched her,
While she sat watching him. "You are not playing
So well—not half so well now—as at first.
You are not so proficient with your cues,
Or with your lines, as when you married me.
I don't see why. You are playing the same part;
And if you are pretending it's a new one,
If you are trying to see yourself a martyr,
You might consider a few famished thousands
Who would go miles tonight to find an egg."
A latterly familiar reek of spirits
Followed his words, and seemed, to Natalie,
To fill the house.

                         "No, I am not a martyr—
I am a fool," she said. "I'm not complaining.
I'm only asking you to go away."

He scowled at her a moment, and came nearer,

Watching her with a smile she did not like.
"For me it's not so easy to go away
From you—sometimes," he said. "You were not made
For me to go away from. If you had been,
I should have gone before, and given you this—
All this you see—to live in. There's a plenty
For me without it, but there's not enough—
Not anywhere—without you. I'll go away,
But that's no reason for not coming back.
That would be rather—rather ridiculous."

He laid his hot hands on her shrinking shoulders,
And would have kissed her, but she sprang from him
Wildly, and stood before him, pale with hate.
"My God!" she cried. "What do you think of me?
What manner of chattel have you made of me?
I know, and I could say. But while I lived
Under your roof with you and ate your bread,
I was a wife. I should have run away,
But was too much a coward, and too weak.
I had been here with everything soft and safe
Too long for that. I had been hidden too long
From all those tiresome things there are to do,
With nothing to do them for. You have your God—
If you have not forgotten him and lost him—
But I have nothing. Do you hear me? Nothing.
I was born spoiled, perhaps—or perhaps not.
You have not spoiled me. You have spoiled yourself.
I should have run away, or should have died,

But never was ready for that—never before.
You reason, I suppose, that without love,
You may as well have my body while it lasts.
Well, it will not last always."

                              "Neither shall I,"
He said, and laughed at her. "He gave you to me,
You said, and you knew then, if I did not,
What he was keeping; and you married me
Because you liked me, and because my love
Was too real to be tortured, and because
There was no better thing for you to do.
You recognize your own remedial words."

"Don't fling that in my face tonight," she said.
"There are things decency says only once.
 You have known that, for you were decent—once.
 Now you are drunk. . . . Why won't you go away!"

Matthias felt a new knife cutting him,
In a new place. He stared, and his lips twisted
Before he laughed. "You said you loved me—once;
And I remember that you said it slowly,
As if it hurt—and probably it did.
But why should it hurt now? You sold yourself
More to your satisfaction and advantage
Than to your disappointment or surprise,
And must have known what you were selling. Love?
I have enough for two. There is more love

In half a minute of my looking at you
Than twenty of you could hold or comprehend.
If you have treasured it for your convenience,
Don't wonder if it seems a bit confused,
Or possibly forgetful. The trouble with you,
And me, and a few millions who are like us,
Is that we live so long to know so little,
And are not willing then to know ourselves.
Where are the mysteries in us that require
So much dramatic fuss? Now we are sorry
For all we've said." He buried her mouth with his,
And held her while she fought and choked and struggled
Till she was free.

        "God—get away from me!"
She cried, and struck his hot face furiously
With an unguided hand that seared with fire
His pride and his belief. Calming her rage,
She saw him there, like a man standing blind,
And found no words to say. There were no words.
And after she was gone he was still there,
Like a man standing dead.

        Hours after that,
Matthias, by dull degrees of realization
That sought oblivion, slowly drank himself
To a dead sleep. When he awoke, the sun
Was in his room, and everything else was there
That should be there; and there was one thing more—

Matthias at the Door

A white thing, a white paper. He reached out,
With fingers trembling, and unfolded it,
Only to find five words. He read them over
Until they had no meaning, and then read them
Until a meaning that was never in them
Pierced him with hope that broke itself in him,
And was no more than pain. Again he read them:
Matthias, I am sorry. Natalie.
Only five words; and while they were so few,
He wondered why those words were so much more
Than nothing at all. At last he rose, not knowing
Why he should rise, or who was alive to care.
He fortified his hope with a brave drink
That once had frightened him, and if no braver,
He was accoutred for a brief endurance
Of what was at the best a long beginning.
He would not ask how long, or of what end.
A stillness like an end was all he found
In Natalie's room; and downstairs it was all
That he found anywhere, till a servant said
That she was last seen going down towards the trees.

Matthias would not eat; he was not well.
Whereat the maid bowed her acknowledgments,
And having left him, smiled. Matthias found
More courage where he found it first, and watched
The twinkling tree-tops while he hesitated.
He would not go, but he should have to go.
Wherever he looked the sunlight tortured him

Part Fourth

With shafts of memory till his eyes were dead
With desolation, and he had no eyes
To meet the pitiless beauty of the world.
But he must go, and he must go alone—
Down to that place. He stumbled as he walked,
As once before, but he moved on, and on,
And down—down among trees and rocks and shadows,
And silence broken only by a brook
Running unseen down there where he must go,
And go alone, knowing what he must find.

V

MATTHIAS, when he saw that Natalie
Was dead, saw nothing else. For a long time
His world, which once had been so properly
And admirably filled with his ambitions,
With Natalie, with his faith, and with himself,
Was only an incredible loneliness,
The lonelier for defeat and recognition.
There was no going back where there was nothing
But memory choked with dust. There was no joy
In gazing at a desert of dead sand
That held above its terrors of endlessness
No more mirages; and there was no refuge
In a retreating faith as unsubstantial
And thankless as a wasted adoration.
There was no reason in such ruin as his,
And no design in any such havoc of pride;
There was no system or serenity,
And no incentive, or there was none for him,
Where there was error without recompense.

It was October now, a chilly Sunday,
And a gray afternoon. Matthias, alone
As always on his desolate veranda,
Sat watching, while he shivered, the bare spikes
That were the tops of oaks and birches growing
Out of a gorge where now he never went.
The place was dead now. Garth and Natalie,
And Timberlake, had made a tomb of it—

Part Fifth

A tomb of life and love, and of his God.
There was a rock down there that Garth had said
Might be the tomb of God, as now it was.
Matthias wondered now if ever his faith
Was more than a traditional convenience
Taken on trust, a plaything of a childhood
That with his ignorance had survived too long.
Let that be as it might, he was lonelier
Than perished life or crumbled love had made him;
Yet he was on an eminence, and would stay there
Until it fell, and carried him down with it.
His pride of unbelief had strength in it
Of a new tonic that must give him strength
Because it was so bitter. There was pride
In bitterness for him who must be proud
Of one thing or another if he would live,
And for Matthias pride was more than life.
So, on a chilly Sunday afternoon,
Alone there with a winter-laden wind
Whirling dead leaves over a darkening floor,
Matthias heard their message and was proud
That he could meet with patience and high scorn
A life without a scheme and to no purpose—
An accident of nameless energies,
Of which he was a part, and no small part.
His blindness to his insignificance
Was like another faith, and would not die.

December went, and with it went a year

That he would never have to live again;
And the new year brought with it nothing new,
Till on a silent evening, in late March,
There was a bell, and then an apparition
Of a lean visitor, wearing clothes almost
As worn-out and as wrinkled as his face.
Matthias rose, while a great wave of joy
Submerged his courtesy and his gratitude,
And he was inarticulate.

                    "Matthias,
You do not have to talk," said Timberlake;
"There's too much talking in the world already.
Give me a drink, and then a beggar's morsel,
And if I'm eligible, a place to sleep.
I have done you no wrong, and little good;
And after that, Matthias, I'm as you see me."
His face and all his wrinkles, and his eyes,
Were smiling at Matthias with a doubt
That held a memory and a wistfulness
Of one who might be welcome, or might not.
"When you have looked me over, and appraised me,
You will be saying without my hearing you,
Matthias, that I'm done. We'll say I am,
And wait for what will happen to the stars
When the news reaches them. I'm tired, Matthias."

He coughed, and held his thin hands to the fire.
Matthias watched him, and again that joy,

Part Fifth

Which had so much of fear in it, possessed him.
For the first time since Natalie had spoken
That evening after Timberlake had gone,
Matthias was not alone. He said that over
Until he smiled and was almost ashamed
Of so great happiness. How much was left
Of Timberlake was all to learn. Meanwhile,
Matthias was not alone.

               When Timberlake
Had warmed himself with fire and food and drink,
And told a story that will not be new
Or old while there is man, poured out more drink,
Chiding Matthias for his abstinence.
"Nothing since Natalie died? That's an odd form
Of eulogy, or commemoration, surely,
For one so measured in his indulgences
As you, Matthias. Do you believe she cares,
Where she is now, what you and I are doing,
Or saying?"

                    "I don't believe she cares, or knows,"
Matthias answered; "and I hope she does n't.
What is there to believe? I believe nothing;
And I am done with mysteries and with gods
That are all gone. Garth was intelligent,
And had found reason, when he told me that."

"So that is what he told you." Timberlake

Matthias at the Door

Smiled at the fire, and thought. "Hold fast, Matthias.
There's not a man who breathes and believes nothing.
So you are done with mysteries. If you are,
You are the one elected and fulfilled
Initiate and emeritus of us all.
You are a man worth a long journeying
Over cold roads to see. I'm not amazed
That you see only folly and false vision
In such a fraudulent and ephemeral
Disguise of life as this." He raised his glass,
And after drinking what was left in it,
Sat musing. "And you tell me this is all
Since Natalie died."

                    "All this, and more than this,
And still more. Natalie told me who I was.
You loved her, Timberlake, and she loved you;
And you must love her still."

                         "I do, Matthias.
Now she is dead, I love her desperately;
And that will do no harm, now that she's dead.
I doubt, with you, if she knows now, or cares;
And if she knows, I dare say she discovers
In my unworthiness of her remembrance
One of those things infinity forgets.
We're more than that, or nothing—as you believe
Since you have torn the veil and have forgotten
Just what it was you saw. Never mind me,

Part Fifth

Matthias. I'm warmer now, and full of thanks
That I can't say for seeing you here again.
Yes, I am warmer now, and reconciled—
Which is important in our preparations.
The time we sigh for what's left out of us
Only gives age to what was always there.
We don't increase ourselves with our regrets
Unless there's action in them. Let us act."
He coughed while he poured out another drink,
And saw Matthias frowning.

                              "It's a blemish,
Matthias, and a maleficence," he said:
"I mean that sad and saurian eye of yours
That's glowering now so cold on my employment.
Now that God's in his grave, where you have laid him,
Are you to set your dogs on Dionysus?
You know those dogs. They were all waiting for me
That afternoon, when they were on your mind.
Though I said little, I could hear them coming,
And not far off. As you observe, they got me,
Tearing the garment of my soul severely,
But not with this that you are giving to me,
To make me warm. It was their teeth, Matthias,
That did the work. This was a balm for that—
For Babylon suddenly fallen and destroyed.
Howl for her; give balm for her wounds, if so
She may be healed. So Jeremiah says—
In substance, or effect. Turn your sad eye

Matthias at the Door

Away from me, Matthias. Be not afraid.
All things that are worth having are perilous,
And have their resident devil, respectively.
There's this that I have here, there's love, pride, art,
Humility, ambition, power and glory,
The kingdom itself, which may come out all right,
And truth. They are all very perilous,
And admirable, so long as there is in them
Passion that knows itself—which, if not hushed,
Is a wise music. Howl, ye ships of Tarshish,
Sang once a Jew. In days of the drunkards of Ephraim,
The Jews had their Ezekiels and Isaiahs,
Solomons, Davids, and a fellow on fire
With Job; for there were howlers in those days.
Now they have power and learning, and quick ears,
And eyes, and hands; yet somehow they are n't howling.
There's mystery there, Matthias. It must be water—
Which is material and insidious,
Prolific in small monsters that are lethal,
And arrogant in its multiform negations.
Our tortured benefits are our worst of demons,
Bleeding us while we sleep."

                              "You are n't asleep,
Timberlake," said Matthias. "I wish you were."
He gazed into the fire and tapped his knees
Uncomfortably. "Your demon's at your service,
Along with anything else of mine you like;
Yet I've an interest in your—your employment.

Part Fifth

You are the only friend that I have left;
And if you die, I shall be here alone.
Here in this world—alone. If that's by chance
A thing significant as another drink—"

"Or two, Matthias. You said two, certainly.
I heard you, and I have a squirrel's ears.
'Good God,' you say? You told me God was buried.
Matthias, you may have buried him alive."

Timberlake honored with an abstinence
That he averred was vain and ostentatious
The fears and wishes of a grateful friend,
And for three days was quiet, save when he coughed
On the fourth morning he reproached himself
While he reproved Matthias: "Your affairs
Are calling you with tongues of gold and silver,
While I'm an obstacle here of no report
Or worldly consequence. I cannot tell you
What infinite progressions and expansions
May or may not be waiting for the end
Of this you see before you in my shape—
Or rather what you don't see. All I can say
To cheer you is that your return tonight
Will find me here, intact and honorable.
You will remember Garth was honorable.
But I'll not follow Garth. I shall not go
Until my name is called. Now, good Matthias,
Go catch a golden fish. You have my word

Of honor, if only for not mentioning it."

The day was harsh and raw, with a wet sky
Preparing coldly to drench everything
With a cold rain. Soiled islands of old snow
Not washed away or melted were not winter,
And unawakening grass that had no color
Was not yet spring. But heedless of a season
That had no name, Matthias in his car
Rode smoothly with a gladness warming him;
For he was not alone. He had one friend—
A frail one, but a friend—a sure possession,
A treasure threatened only with a fear
That having found and sheltered it so late,
He might not have it long. But worry for that,
Or worry too soon, would be a thanklessness
For one who was safe now in a warm house,
With all his economic woes behind him,
With books to read, and with a smouldering hope
To guard and to restore. He was not old.
His wrinkles were not years; they were a life,
Written for all to see and none to read.
"We are not old at fifty any longer,"
Matthias thought; "and there's a place for him
As long as I'm alive, and afterwards—
If so it is to be. I do not know him,
And never shall. No man has known another
Since men were born. It is enough to know
That he is in my house, and is my friend."

Part Fifth

The swollen sky broke in the afternoon,
And it was raining while Matthias rode
Through storm and early darkness to a house
That for so long had been the tomb of life.
He thought of that, and smiled as he went in
To find a waiting friend who was not there.
No one had seen him, or knew where he was.
He had been sitting mostly by the fire,
And watching it. They had not thought of him
As anything stranger than a quiet person,
Who coughed too much, and had considerate words
When there were words to say. For an hour or two
Perhaps, before it rained, he was not there.
If he was not upstairs and in his room,
He must be gone. Now it was five o'clock,
And for an hour or more a deathly rain
Had deluged all outside with a cold flood
That would have chilled and driven a lunatic
To shelter; and the man was not in the house.
There was no longer any doubt of that.
He was somewhere; and he was not in the house.

At six o'clock Matthias and two men,
Arrayed against a tempest, went with torches
Down to the one place that was darkly left
As an abysmal possibility —
Or rather went halfway down. There was no need
Of going farther; for where Garth had found
Matthias, they found Timberlake, dumb, drenched,

Exhausted, and with only his eyes at first
To say that he was living. When he spoke,
It was to cough and whisper, while he smiled,
That he could go no higher, and was sorry
For being a fool. That was like Timberlake;
So like him that Matthias could almost
Be glad there for the rain that washed his tears
Out of existence before Timberlake
Could see them—as if pride stronger than death
Was his, like Natalie's folly.

                              The next day,
Timberlake, with Matthias watching him,
Lay waiting for the fiends that were assembling
To fight with him for breath. "I did not come
For this, Matthias." Half whispering, he said it,
Implying grimly that it mattered little
What he had come for. "I sat yesterday
There by the fire and saw Natalie in it—
And there was Garth. I saw them both down there,
Where each had gone alone, for the last time.
I saw that place where Natalie was alone,
Until you found her there. I would not see her,
In there, but she was calling. She was calling
For me, for the last time. And I went down,
Say what you will. 'She was in there,' I said,
And sat before the place where she had been,
Trying to say that she had not been there.
I sat there till it rained, and while it rained,

Part Fifth

Because I could not move. I was too cold.
Too much of me was dead for me to care
Whether I came up out of there or not.
I was not thinking of how cold I was,
But rather of you and Natalie, Matthias,
And of what we had made of our three lives—
Or life had made of us. It seemed a waste
Of more than should be lost, until I thought
Of nature's way and of how small we are
In our performances, and how infinite
In our futilities and our ignorances.
They are as many and various as we are,
Always in our degrees, which are not ours
To choose, yet may be ours to recognize
And occupy more profitably—sometimes.
If I have made my best of my not much—
And God knows you believe that I have not,
Matthias—I am sorry it was no better.
You saved me from the fire; and you saved more,
Conceivably, than you see. There should have been
Far more for you to save; and why there was n't
Is one of those long questions we don't answer.
So do not ask me why so many of us
Are more like sketches of ourselves, half done
By nature, and forgotten in her workshop,
Than like a fair or tolerable fulfilment
Of her implied intention. Implications
Of more than is revealed in our defeats
Are targets always for the many who trust

And emulate, and crown with confidence,
A self-enveloping uniformity
Of compromise. That's how the world was made
Before my lost omniscience came too late.
Why are we as we are? Don't ask, Matthias.
Why do we come to nothing who have more,
We'll say, than most? What is our value here
Unless we fit? To make a mould that fits us,
You'd like to say, Matthias, but are n't going to.
Read a few years of history, and you'll see
The stuff is not so pliable as all that.
If it were so, we should all be each other—
So great that nature would be on her knees,
Which is not nature's natural attitude.
Why are we as we are? We do not know.
Why do we pay so heavily for so little?
Or for so much? Or for whatever it is?
We do not know. We only pay, and die.
To a short-sighted and earth-hindered vision
It would seem rather a waste, but not to mine.
I have found gold, Matthias, where you found gravel,
And I can't give it to you. I feel and see it,
But you must find it somehow for yourself.
It's not negotiable. You have to find it—
Or say it must find you. Even you, Matthias."

He paused, and coughed, until Matthias turned
His eyes away, and sighed. "Forgive my not
Remembering, Timberlake. You must be still.

Part Fifth

There will be time for this."

                              "God knows, Matthias,
Whether there will or not, or if it matters.
If I've done one thing well, I have not meddled,
Until today, with men's inheritances
And acquisitions. But men like you, Matthias,
Believe that if you stumble the world trembles.
Try to believe now, as a friendly favor
To me, that it does nothing of the sort.
If you had eyes inside you, and you may,
To read a little further into your book—
Well, you would be surprised at what is there
For you to find. If it had not been there,
I might have hated you for saving me,
When we were young, out of that burning house.
There was a price for that, which I have paid
As well as I was able. Natalie paid,
And you are paying still. We are like stairs
For one another's climbing, and are never
Quite told which way it is that we are going
While we are climbing higher, or think we are.
I have not always thought so; but you have,
Matthias, and I have watched you going up
While you were going down. You are down now
As far as you will go—if you remember
That you are like a book with pages in it
You have not read, and cannot read in the dark.
Some of us would be happier in the dark,

Matthias at the Door

As you have been, and cannot be again.
More darkness would have been a balm for me,
But not a cure. There is no cure for self;
There's only an occasional revelation,
Arriving not infrequently too late.
For me it was too early — which is granted,
Sometimes, to the elected and the damned.
I don't suppose that I was all a fool,
Or that I was all bad. There have been worse
Who have aroused more reverence and more noise,
And shown more colors to the common view,
And I'm at peace with them. If I whined now
For benefits that I may have lost or wasted,
I should lose only more. Spare me all twaddle
Of what I might have been; for you don't know,
And would still be Matthias if you did.
No estimate or retrospect of me
Will save you now. There's a nativity
That waits for some of us who are not born.
Before you build a tower that will remain
Where it is built and will not crumble down
To another poor ruin of self, you must be born.
You are not old, Matthias; you are so young
That you see nothing in fate that takes away
Your playthings but a curse, and a world blasted,
And stars you cannot reach that have no longer
A proper right to shine. And that's no way
For me to say it to a friend who cares.
A friend who takes me in out of the cold,

Part Fifth

And sees me on my way, and will be sorry,
Merits a more communicable reward
Than talk of towers that will be built sometime,
Or of lives wasted that will not be lost—
Not even if thrown away. Say to yourself
That if some wreck that was not Timberlake
Were telling you to go back, you would arise
Refreshed and better for having strangled him.
Don't listen to me, Matthias, for I'm tired;
And I don't half believe what I am saying."

"Yes, Timberlake, you believe it," said Matthias;
"And why not? I don't know that we are wasted.
Since Natalie spoke to me when you had gone,
That evening, I've had no knowledge, or belief.
Perhaps I never had it. Why do you smile?
And why do you never mention Natalie?"

Timberlake said, "I mentioned her, Matthias.
I mentioned when I came that now she's dead,
I love her desperately. You must have heard.
You were supposed to hear."

                              "Yes, I heard that,"
Matthias answered. "And I am never to know
What my life was with her. My knowledge fell
One day, and broke like glass on a stone floor."

"Don't try to know, Matthias," Timberlake said,

Matthias at the Door

And held out a weak hand. "Say that's all over,
And that illumination would light nothing
Where there is only dust. Don't ask, Matthias.
A happy woman may be understood,
Or near enough, but there is no man living
With eyes or intuitions to interpret
A woman hiding pain. Don't try, Matthias."

Again, with his blue eyes and all his wrinkles,
Timberlake smiled. Matthias looked away
And heard him coughing. All that night he heard him,
And for three days and nights heard nothing else,
While doctors came and went and shook their heads
At Timberlake, who, having outlived surprise,
Had seen them when they fancied he saw nothing.

VI

MATTHIAS in his dreams would have a glimpse
Of Natalie sometimes, but never a word
Until he found himself alone with her
One night in regions he could name as only
Nowhere on earth. Natalie came to him
Robed all in gold—a film of heavenly wealth
To make him gasp. There was gold everywhere.
Matthias had loved gold for what it gave him,
But never had asked for this. Natalie laughed:
"I know, Matthias. I know all your thoughts,
As you will soon know mine. They are good thoughts.
Everything here is good, as your God made it.
You died, Matthias; and now you are in heaven,
With me, for ever; and I shall never change.
My soul and body are yours, and will be yours,
And always, which is now. There is no time
To make us old, for there is nothing but love,
Nothing but you and me." He felt her breath
Warm on his face, and her warm body clinging
To his until it seemed a part of him;
And he was trembling for the wonder of it
When she began, still in his arms, to shrivel
And change, unspeakably and abominably,
While all about him became dark and foul,
And only darker while infernal fires
Lighted what once was gold. Natalie's face
Was now a demon's, and her breath was fire;
And she was like a skeleton strangling him.

[81]

Matthias at the Door

"You are in hell, Matthias," she was saying;
"Your God has changed his mind"—when suddenly
He was in darkness that he slowly felt,
And knew, and recognized. He was awake.
He was awake, but he still heard her laughing
As woman cannot laugh. He was awake,
Somewhere, and he was on his feet somewhere;
For he was standing in the dark, alone,
With a sweat chilling him. He groped a little,
Only to find black air, till gradually
Blackness became a room that was not his,
With outlines in it of still things that once
Were Natalie's. He had come there asleep,
To find her in a dream of heaven, and then
To lose her in another dream of hell.
His life with Natalie had been like that,
He thought; yet he could think no ill of her,
Though she had struck him. He could not forget
The blow, and he could not forget his love,
Which had been real, if blind and unreturned,
With Natalie a stranger in his house,
And in his arms. But Natalie was gone,
And there was little use in saying that over.
Trying to sleep once more, he found himself
Still saying it, over and over, against reason
And against fate. The foodless luxury
Of a dry truth was all it had for him;
And it was all that life had while he felt
The memories of a nightmare stinging him

Part Sixth

To a sick wakefulness. There was no sleep
Till daylight came, and then there was so little
That it was easier not to wait for more.
For days the taint of that perfidious dream
Was like a smell of death following him —
A death that would not die. At last it faded,
Leaving him as he was before — alone.

A longer loneliness, with no friend coming
This time, and none to come, compelled Matthias
Half-heartedly to search the darkness in him,
Hoping to find surprise where Timberlake
Had said it lived in unsuspected ambush,
Patient and there to wait. But no surprise
Had yet revealed itself except a small
And useless one of his not finding any.
All he could find was an unsatisfied
Conviction of no room for anything new —
A certainty that had concealed in it
Somewhere a question that was like a midge
In a man's eye. He sought for it in books
That were like heavy keys for doors not his
To open, and doubted if they fitted even
The doors of those who had invented them.
Some of the newest of them had already
Richer accumulations of more rust,
Matthias fancied, than the oldest of them;
And there was nothing in any of them for him.
The best of them were moonshine without light,

Matthias at the Door

Or news of an ingenious mechanism
That must have built itself mysteriously
And infinitely out of infinite nothing.
His brain ached, and he went back to himself,
As he had gone a thousand times before,
To see what there was there, still hoping faintly
To find surprise. But all he found was doubt,
Insoluble and impregnable as ever,
And the same man. He must be the same man,
For he was still Matthias. If he had built
His life like a tall tower to see it fall,
There were no failures in his masonry,
Nor in the safe precision of his plan;
He had built, with all his foresight and selection,
On undivined and insecure foundations
Deeper than all security and precaution
Had whispered there was reason to explore.
He saw it lying about him, shafts and arches,
And shattered walls, in fragments on the ground,
And for no fault of his. The only eyes
He had were those that his inheritance
Had given to him, and he had seen with them
Only what he might see. He saw that now,
And asked his eyes, hoping there was no answer,
Where they had seen a ruin like this before,
And turned them on himself to ask again
What they were seeing. It was the same man—
A man with nothing left but money and pride,
Neither of which was worth his living for,

If there was nothing else. To live alone,
A captive in a world where there were none
Who cared for him, and none for whom he cared,
Was a dark sentence and might be a long one.
Digesting that, he thought of Garth saying once:
"You'd save a man from drowning, or from burning,
And tell him then that he was not worth saving—
Unless you liked him. I like you, Matthias,
And so does Timberlake; and God knows why.
We are outside the wall that you have built
Around yourself and Natalie—or I am.
Timberlake may climb over or crawl through,
Once in a while, and you had better let him."

"Well, Garth, I should be glad enough to see you
Tonight, if you were coming to my door,"
Matthias thought; "and I might say to you
A few things more to your desire and liking
Than many I may have said. You will not come,
And would not if you could—if Timberlake
Saw truth before he died. If he was dreaming,
We are all dreaming, and it's all the same
To him now, and to you. When towers are fallen,
The tallest are no loftier than the lowest.
Falling so far, they drive the ruin only
A little deeper into original earth.
Tonight I'm not so free with your last folly
As I was while I gazed at my tall tower
Before it fell, and was so ready to fall.

Matthias at the Door

No, Garth, I'm not so sure you were a fool,
Now that I see you in a clearer light.
It was undignified, but not ignoble."

Matthias did not know that in his garden
There were some perilous seeds of sympathy
That he had found and planted, unaware
Of what they were or what they might conceal,
Until another Sunday afternoon
Found him, in August, watching the same tops
Of oaks and birches growing out of a gorge
That held so many memories. The veranda
Where he was sitting was a silent place,
And so was the whole house. With his permission,
All its inhabitants were away somewhere,
Leaving him like that last man in the world
Whom he had seen in fancy—as in truth
He saw the last man living in his world,
Which he was leaving. From the shining tops
Of those familiar and indifferent trees,
He turned and looked into a lonely chair—
Natalie's chair. She was not in it now,
And never was in it. There was a woman in it,
Once, and a woman he was never to know.
He was never to know anything. He was lost.
He had explored himself so many times
To find surprise where there was only darkness
That he was tired of darkness. He was alone,
And he was tired of that. He was alive,

With pride for company, and now pride was tired
Of groping with Matthias among shadows,
Where for three years they had been prisoners.
Matthias was a man who must have light,
Or darkness that was rest and certainty,
With no fool-fire of an unfuelled faith
Invading it and losing its own spark,
Such as it was. Matthias was alone,
And there was only loneliness before him,
Because he was Matthias, and had failed.
He would have prayed for less intelligence,
But there were no prayers in him any longer.
It was too late. He looked at his calm hand,
And saw death lying there. "Why not?" he said
To Pride, who said, "It is undignified,
But not ignoble." Matthias winced at that,
And said to Pride, "You think I am afraid?"
"No, you are not afraid; you are Matthias,"
Pride answered; and Matthias, with a sigh
Of satisfaction, lay back in his chair
So comfortably that comfort was itself
Surprise. He knew that he was not afraid,
And there were days enough. There were too many,
If many of them were to be like today.

Sighing, he wished that he might hear the steps
Of Timberlake again and see him coming,
With all his wrinkles and his twinkling eyes,
Which had seen farther and found more, somewhere,

Than his were ever to find. With all his waste.
And his uncounted losses, Timberlake
Had died the richer man, having found gold
Where there was only gravel for Matthias;
And that was strange. Timberlake was a ruin,
But he was not alone. He was always a ruin,
But never alone. Matthias had felt that
From childhood, and was feeling it today
So finally that a waiting for more days
Disheartened him, although there was no haste.
Besides, he was too indolent to care,
And one day meant another. Garth had said
Sunday was good, and had not waited for it.
Garth had done well. Why should Matthias wait
For Monday?

He was asking, with no answer,
While hours went by and a long afternoon
Became a twilight and an end of time —
A twilight, or a darkness, where Matthias
Could see confronting him, invitingly,
A dark Egyptian door. Now it was closed,
And silent, but a touch would open it,
Giving him entrance. He would leave all behind
That he was glad to leave; and once inside,
There was to be no coming out of there.
It was as easy and as ordinary
As going to bed. There was no hesitation
Longer defeating him; there were no doubts

Part Sixth

Delaying him. His hand was on the door,
Which he felt moving, slowly, when a voice
Within said, warningly, "Not yet, Matthias."

There was decision and authority
Not native in that voice. Matthias frowned,
But he was not surprised. It was like Garth
To say that, and to be there in his way,
Matthias thought, though he could not say then
Why it was like him. "Garth, is it you," he said,
"Telling me I should wait? Why should I wait?
If you knew all that I have known of waiting,
Alone, you would be glad to let me in.
Whose power is yours to say what I shall do?
What if I show you that my power is mine?"

"Not yet, Matthias. No matter what you do,
You are not coming. A way was found for me
To meet you here and say you are not coming.
You cannot die, Matthias, till you are born.
You are down here too soon, and must go back.
Don't be annoyed, or be disquieted,
Or more than necessarily surprised
At any change. You will still be yourself
When you are born. There is no cure for self;
There's only an occasional—"

                              "Yes, I know it.
So I have heard before, from Timberlake.

[89]

Matthias at the Door

Where is he now? And where is Natalie?
Why are they not with you, to meet me here
And tell me to go back? Where are they, Garth?"

"What the world had for them is theirs, Matthias,
Wherever they may be now. They are not here,
And I shall soon be gone. But you were coming,
And I am saying that you are going back.
I'm sorry to dishearten or to vex you,
But you might still go back if you came in.
It's all a matter of seeing which way we go;
And it's imperative that you shall be born,
Whether you will or not, before you die.
I am an emissary of the shadow
In this, Matthias, and I'm nothing more.
I see a little, but I'm still in the dark."

"But this is folly. This is all folly, Garth —
Like some occasional words I may have said
Of your procrastinations and shortcomings.
They were so easy to say, that — well, I said them;
And I am sorry. Your lessons were too hard.
Now I begin to see that your instructions
In the world's exigencies were not mine."

"Terrestrial exigencies are the devil,
Matthias, and others exist; and other devils.
Your generous language, and its implications,
Although a little delayed, will not be wasted.

Part Sixth

Nothing is wasted, though there's much misused —
Like you and me, Matthias, who failed together,
Each in a personal way. You, having more
To fail with, failed more thoroughly and abjectly,
But that was not the end. I shall go on,
Where you'll not follow me. You will go back,
Where I'll not follow you. And in that fashion
We shall go on unconsciously together,
And consciously apart, to the same end.
It's all a matter of our not going too fast."

"And what same end is that? I am down here
To find the only end, and you forbid it —
Or say it is forbidden. Who says it is?
What if I push my way in while you tell me
Where I shall go? There can be nothing worse
For me in there than death; and if I'm here
For that, why should I listen or hesitate?
So far as I know, you are only a voice
Between me and oblivion. I have come
Too far through dark realities to be scared
At last by buried voices. You are dead,
And the dead cannot hurt."

                              "There's no regret,
Matthias, with a sorrier sting in it
Than for a word that cannot be withdrawn.
The dead have weapons to pierce all defiance
Of pride and vanity, which are flimsy shields

Matthias at the Door

For those who must remember. You know that,
Or you would not be fumbling at this door
To find an entry. Push with all your power,
Matthias, and we shall see how strong you are.
I shall not hinder you. The door does that
To all who are not ready enough to move it,
Or are not desperate enough to break it.
It moved for you a little to let you hear
My voice, but you will see it moves no more.
I broke it once, and I am here to meet you.
The others are not here. Make what you will
Of that," said Garth.

           "Natalie broke it once,"
Matthias said. "Could her poor little hands
Do heavier work than mine? Where is she now?
What does she say of me? You will not answer."

"I cannot tell you where she is, Matthias.
She is not here. Her way was hers, not mine.
Make what you will of that. There are differences
Of desperation as there are of ruin
And uselessness; and you have found this door
Too soon. It will not open, and would be here
If you should wreck it. It's a peculiar door;
And when you are assured it will not open,
You will not come until your name is called."

"I have heard that. There's more of Timberlake

Part Sixth

In you than of yourself. Is it you, Garth?
It is your voice."

"No matter whose voice it is,
Matthias. It may be yours. It may be Cæsar's.
All voices are one voice, with many tongues
To make it inexpressible and obscure
To us until we hear the voice itself.
We are prisoners now and pupils in a school
Where often our best rewards appear to us
To be our punishments. There's no escape.
To sleep with earth between you and the sun
Is not escape from earth, or from the sun.
It seems a mystery that so many should live
Who are not born, but that's the infinite way,
And one that is not altered or improved
By protest or denial, or by rebellion.
It's an old-fashioned way, older than fashion,
And it will serve your need better than any.
You have not yet begun to seek what's hidden
In you for you to recognize and use.
There's more of you for you to find, Matthias,
Than science has found yet, or may find soon.
Science that blinds its eyes incessantly
With a new light that fades and leaves them aching,
Whatever it sees, will be a long time showing
To you, Matthias, what you have striven so hard
To see in the dark. You will not see it there,
Though you may find it there if a door opens.

Matthias at the Door

Not this door, but another one in yourself."

"In me, in you, and all to the same end,"
Replied Matthias, with a rueful breath
Of weariness that was answered amiably,
And with no accusation or resentment:
"You will be happier to forget the end,
Or more than revelation or conviction
Tell you to see, and to make what you may
Of your apportioned means. The end will wait
For all your most magnificent and protracted
Progressions and expansions, and be still
Sufficiently far away."

                    "Why do you laugh,
When you had better tell me," said Matthias,
"If these untold progressions and expansions
Of yours, or Timberlake's, begin with us,
Or if worms, armadillos, and hyenas
Have them as well. Where may the soul begin?
And why not grass? There's mystery living in grass
As dark as any in me."

                    "Language, Matthias.
With a few finite and unfinished words
That are the chips of brief experience,
You restless and precipitate world-infants
Would build a skiff to circumnavigate
Infinity, and would find it, if you could,

Part Sixth

No more sufficient or more commodious
Or comprehensive in its means and habit
Than a confused, confined phenomenon
Prisoned within a skull, with knowledge in it.
There's not much knowledge in it, and less wisdom.
How are you sure that some of you, Matthias,
May not be grass? And why not armadillos?
Men have done well with coverings hard as theirs.
I have seen men with more hyena in them
Than man; and I've seen others with more worm.
If you could know, Matthias, you would be free.
But you are far from knowing, and are not free;
You are not even free to open this door,
Or broken enough to break it. Only defeat
Born of disintegration and despair
Does that, Matthias. Your pride would only break
Its hands, and be ashamed to see them bleeding
After so blind a fight. You will go back
To build another tower — a safer one
This time, and one for many to acclaim
And to enjoy. It will be yours to build —
As towers, in your opinion, should be built;
It will be yours to admire while it is rising,
And yours to dedicate, when it has risen,
To whom it shall serve best. You have no friends,
And when you have seen deeper you may learn
That friends, for you, might be impediments,
Or luxuries, or counsellors in the way
Of your convictions and your certainties.

Matthias at the Door

You will have occupation all your days,
With none to tell you this or that about it,
Or how it should be done. It will be done
About as your desire and your decision
May visualize and sanction its emergence
Out of a slumbering thought. You are not old,
And will be younger still when you are born.
Most of us are half-born, with only self
To cheer us with a promise of importance
Until it is all over—in appearance—
And one by one we're down here at this door,
Some frightened, some indifferent, some content,
And a few frantic, or experimental—
Like you, Matthias—in anticipation.
Forget that, and anticipate your tower;
And sometime, when you see it and have leisure
To look away from it, you may remember,
And gratefully, that you came once down here,
Where I came first, and Natalie not long after.
Your right remembrance of her will be gladness
That she is not here now, waiting outside,
And fearful to come in. You would not see her
Out there with her face white and her hands shaking,
And all to do again. She was a creature
Caught in a trap she thought was only a cage
Of many comforts with an open door—
Until she knew; and she is farther now
From you and your concerns and preparations
Than words of yours have eyes or feet or wings

To follow her. She wants no following now,
And no recall. Say that she was not wasted,
And you may see your tower a little stronger
For no vast sacrifice. And for myself,
You will excuse a few diseased remarks
That made a mean farewell. I was not there,
Matthias; it was mostly fear and envy
That you observed and heard—fear of myself
And of what I was doing, envy of you
And of what you had done. We did not know—
Not then—how little that was. Good-bye, Matthias,
And let the best of us that you remember
Serve as it may. The worst is good oblivion.
There's a ship waiting for you; and when dawn
Begins to let you know, you will see then
That you are outward bound, with all your ruins
And all your old mistakes on board with you—
With you, and your regrets, and your possessions,
And with yourself, and all that makes a tower.
There may still be surprise. You are so far
From sure tonight that you and all before you,
And after you, are nothing, and here for nothing,
That you are curious. You are smiling now.
Yes, I can see in the dark. Good-bye, Matthias

Matthias, in a light that was a darkness
More than a light, saw the door shut itself
Inexorably; and there was only silence,
Saying he must go back. There was no door

There now, and there was nothing for him to see.
There was a cloak of night that covered him
So heavily that he felt the weight of it.
He held his eyes wide open to see that door
Again, but all was black. He might have been
Buried and dead, if he had not been breathing.
He breathed, and moved, and slowly satisfied
His doubtful sense of being that he was alive,
And that he was awake. He had been awake
Like this in Natalie's room, after that dream,
But he was not there now. He moved his hands,
And then his arms, but they found only darkness
That was too cold and heavy to be in his house.
He was not there; he was in no man's house.
He took a searching step and felt dark earth
Under his foot; and suddenly he heard
A tinkling in the night like a small music
That had been always and would always be,
And was a brook; and there was only one brook
Running like that. With both his hands before him,
He groped a short way forward and was halted
By rock that he could see with his eyes open
Or closed. He was down there where Natalie
And Garth and Timberlake had been before him;
And they were all gone now. He had come down
To follow them, and found he was not wanted.
He must go back again; he must be born,
And then must live; and he who had been always
So promptly served, and was to be a servant,

Part Sixth

Must now be of some use in a new world
That Timberlake and Garth and Natalie
Had strangely lived and died to find for him.
He had no friends, and his not having them now
Might be as well for him and his new tower.
To say that it was his and see it rising,
Would be enough. And while he saw it rising,
It would be his; and it would be himself
Behind him when he died. Even Timberlake
Would grant him that; and if his eyes agreed,
And all his wrinkles, they would do no harm.

Groping away, with his hands out before him,
And his feet going cautiously, Matthias
Moved as a blind man moves, with memory
Guiding him as it might, until he found
An unseen place to rest. The night was cold,
And in the darkness was a feel of death,
But in Matthias was a warmth of life,
Or birth, defending and sustaining him
With patience, and with an expectancy
That he had said would never in life again
Be his to know. There were long hours to wait,
And dark hours; and he met their length and darkness
With a vast gratitude that humbled him
And warmed him while he waited for the dawn.